AF480979

This book is dedicated to
Katherine Meyers and all the
caregivers who love and nurture
children with Down syndrome.

– Sally

A special thank you to Trevin
for not only being a part of
the story, but also for his
drawings of his family that have
been included in the book!

My name is **Trevin** and I have a story to tell.
Now listen closely,
SO I DON'T HAVE TO YELL.

Five years ago my brother, Lincoln was born.
He made us a family of SIX.

Our family is now 3 boys and 3 girls.
We're a happy, silly mix!

But **Lincoln's** birth wasn't normal.
I'm not even sure what normal really means.

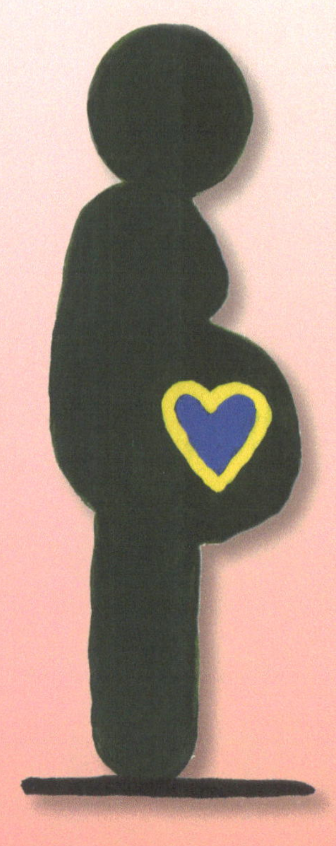

Lincoln has **DOWN SYNDROME.**
My parents told me that it's just part of his genes.

Lincoln's no longer a baby.
Every day he's growing TALLER and getting older.

But even though he's still little,
he's teaching me great things!
Like life is best when
you're bolder.

He's teaching me
TO BE BOLD
in many ways...

Lesson #1:
BE BOLD
BY LEARNING
NEW THINGS!

Our bodies are made up of
BUILDING BLOCKS.

Each building block is called a **CELL**.

Inside each cell are **CHROMOSOMES**.
And oh, the stories
those things tell!

Chromosomes could tell your body to **GROW QUITE TALL**.
They could tell your hair to be **BLONDE, RED, OR BLACK**.
They could make you
RUN REALLY FAST.

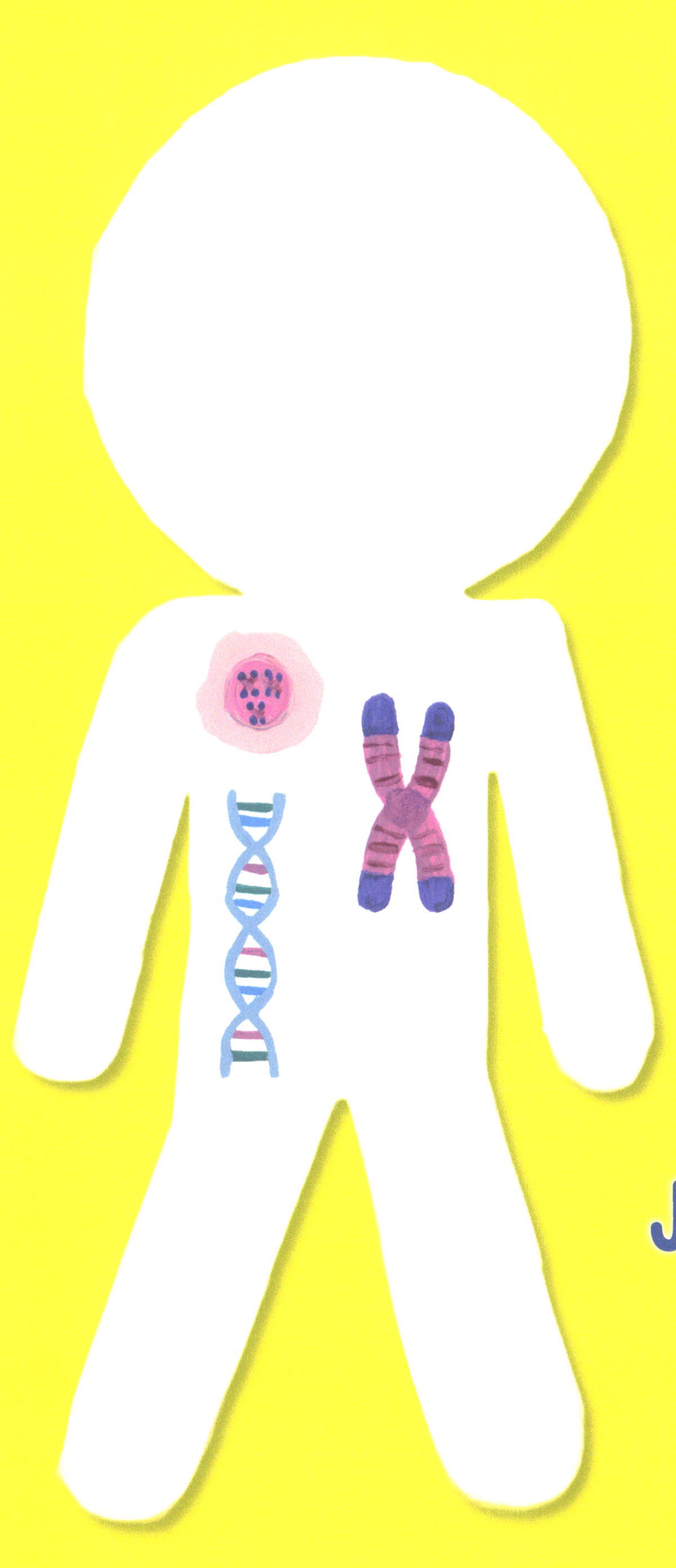

Or even make you **LAUGH** like your Great Uncle Jack.

Most of us have **46** chromosomes in each cell. But **Lincoln** has **47**. He's got **1 EXTRA CHROMOSOME**.

And it's helping me learn more about

JESUS and **HEAVEN**.

People with **47 CHROMOSOMES** have
DOWN SYNDROME.
Down syndrome isn't an illness, or even a disease.
It's just part of who Lincoln is.
So listen up carefully, please.

Lincoln may look a little different.
He learns in special ways, too.
He works extra hard to make his muscles strong.
He's just a little different from me and you.

Lincoln is still young and small,
But he's becoming my **GREATEST TEACHER**.
He taught me about Down syndrome,
Now I'm a smarter creature.

BE BOLD BY BEING KIND!

Our family likes to play games and sing.
Oh, and we love to dance!
We're one family, but each one of us is different.
We are more than what you may see at first glance.

I really like to draw.
In fact, I love to work on my art.
It's how I express myself.
It shows what's in my heart.

I like to draw pictures of cars, animals, and people.
And when I draw people, that's when I really see.
THAT GOD MADE US ALL DIFFERENT.
We're all as different as can be!

We come in different colors and SIZES.
And some of us talk in different ways.
And this just makes me think...
**WE SHOULD USE OUR DIFFERENCES
TO BRING GOD PRAISE!**

God gave us each a special gift, or skill.
I can draw. That's what I like to do best.
Lincoln makes everyone smile.
He brings joy and gives life some zest.

No matter what you look like, or what your skills may be.
There's one thing we should always keep in mind.
WE SHOULD TREAT EVERYONE WITH RESPECT.
WE SHOULD ALWAYS BE KIND.

Lincoln is still young and small,
But he's becoming my greatest teacher.
He taught me that we're all different
with special gifts to share.
NOW I'M A KINDER CREATURE.

Lesson #3:

BE BOLD BY BEING GENEROUS!

Lincoln smiles every day. He brings joy everywhere he goes.
He's a giver that's for sure.
FOOD
From his head to his toes.

Lincoln gives love and joy.
He shines his light every day.
He shares all that he is.
He makes each day better, in his own way.

No matter the circumstances.
Be it a pandemic, chaos, or fear.
He brings JOY to others.
He loves all who are near.

Lincoln gives more than he takes.
His generosity knows no bounds.
He's teaching me more about sharing.
His love comes from higher grounds.

Lincoln is still young and small,
But he's becoming MY GREATEST TEACHER.
He taught me to share my gifts and to just be myself.
Now I'm a more generous creature.

Lincoln has taught me to always be willing to
LEARN NEW THINGS
And to be kind and generous, too.

The greatest teachers in life might be the ones you least suspect.

They'll make you
a better
YOU!